Primix Publishing
11620 Wilshire Blvd
Suite 900, West Wilshire Center, Los Angeles, CA, 90025
www.primixpublishing.com
Phone: 1-800-538-5788

Published by Primix Publishing: 03/14/2024

ISBN: 979-8-89194-108-3(sc)
ISBN: 979-8-89194-109-0(e)

Library of Congress Control Number: 2024901998

RACISM AND GOD'S INVITATION

Systemic Racism plagues our society and distorts the church's ministry. Our faith invites us to move beyond
DENIAL AND GUILT

Stephen McCutchan

RACISM AND PRIVILEGE

How does the Christian church respond to the systemic racism that plagues our society? How do we faithfully respond to the fact that predominantly White congregations[1] have been infected by a cancer of racism that infuses their life and distorts their experience of the Gospel as they practice their ministry within the culture of the United States of America. Rather than react in either denial or paralyzing guilt, I believe that the recognition of this reality offers immense promise for our understanding the saving nature of the church in our society.

In examining this situation, it is helpful to begin with some clarification of terms. First, the term racism refers to a condition that applies primarily to White[n] people. Racism is distinct from, although related to, prejudice. Prejudice can be part of any person's attitude. It is, as the word implies, a prejudgment that negatively reflects on one's attitude towards a situation, people, or person. Often people make prejudicial judgments about categories of people based on religion, skin color, dress, age, or size.

In preparation for understanding the distinction between prejudice and racism, it is helpful to understand that prejudice can work for and against people. For example, I am white, male, over six feet tall, and have no obvious physical abnormalities. I do not have to be consciously prejudiced against any person who does not have those qualifications to recognize that I have benefited from privileges granted to me by society because of those characteristics. I not only benefit from such privileges but, despite my desire for a fairer and more just world, I am not inclined to refuse such benefits in pursuit of the cause of justice and fairness.

At the same time, people's prejudice can work against a person. I might see a person dressed in dirty, smelly clothes and assume that the person is illiterate, lazy, and perhaps dangerous. There might be a number of other explanations for the person's condition, but my prejudgment hinders, and many times prevents, further information from being gathered that might alter my perception of that person.

Such prejudgments or prejudicial conclusions are frequently made about people who are distinctly different from us. In this country, race is a major factor that feeds such prejudice. Racism combines prejudice with power. Racism includes the prejudice, whether conscious or unconscious, that people of color are in some way inferior to Caucasian people. Have you ever met a Caucasian person whose basic assumption was that Black people as a race were superior to Whites? Many Black people have prejudices with respect to Caucasian people, but the difference is that the structures of society give Caucasians the advantage.

THE COLOR OF BREAD

Some of the dynamics of this reality are captured in a scene from a play entitled *The Color of Bread*. The scene takes place at an officers' retreat of a consciously biracial church. The officers have convened to respond to a complaint that they have received that their food pantry has been reflecting a prejudice in the way that they deliver food to the poor. As we join the discussion, they are trying to understand the dynamics of racism.

For purpose of identification, I will place a (B) before the characters of African-American descent and a (W) before those of Caucasian descent. The conversation is already in progress, and one of the Caucasian members has just expressed the hope that we would all learn to live together without always evaluating our relationships in terms of race.

(B) **Reverend Evan White**: "That's a nice ideal, but the ugly reality of the world keeps imposing itself on us. As Christians we may not be of this world, but we are certainly fully mired in it."

(W) **Reverend Carol Black**: "What do you mean, Evan?"

(B) **Harry**: "What he means is that we live in a world of power."

(B) **Ralph**: "You can be as nice as you want to be to me, but you always have the option to withhold that niceness."

(W) **Shirley**: "Wait just one blessed minute. Don't we all have the same choices to be nice or not nice to whomever we want to? That is certainly what I try to tell all my staff at the agency."

(B) **Felicia**: "That's true, Shirley, but the difference is power. When you stop being nice to one of your staff, you still have the power. When they stop being nice to you, they can quickly be left out in the cold."

(W) **Al**: "What do you mean, power? I wish I did have some power. I'd like to make a lot of changes. But frankly, I don't control much of anything"

(B) **Harry**: "In one sense that is true, Al, but in a larger sense it is not."

(W) **Al**: "What do you mean?"

(B) **Harry**: "Well, think about it. If suddenly tomorrow all Blacks decided they didn't like how Whites were treating them, big whoopee—the world goes on. But if Whites decided they didn't like how Blacks were treating them, hey, the Congress could pass new laws of segregation tomorrow, the banks could call in loans, the grocers could stop selling food, Black kids could get kicked out of school, and we would have no recourse."

(W) **Al**: "Oh, come on, give us some credit for the progress we've made. With all our civil rights laws, nothing like that could ever happen today."

(B) **Felicia**: "Al, sweetheart, you've been teaching those students all those good feeling lessons during Black History Month and you've done forgot that most of us have to live in the real world the other eleven months of the year too."

(W) **Jerry**: "Heh! Wait a minute. I teach my children about Black history and how to treat each other fairly. What's wrong with that?"

(B) **Harry** rises and walks over to a mirror leaning against a wall. "Come over here for a moment, Jerry." Jerry gets up and walks over towards where Harry is standing. "Look in this mirror and tell me what you see, Jerry."

(W) **Jerry**: "I'm not sure what you mean. I just see me."

(B) **Harry**: "You're right, Jerry. Most White people look in a mirror and just see themselves. I'll bet it never occurs to you to notice what color you are."

(W) **Shirley**, joining them at the mirror, "What I notice is some new gray hairs, but I admit I have never been conscious of the color of my skin."

(B) **Reverend Evan White**: "That's because you just assume that being white is normal."

(W) **Shirley**: "You mean you don't assume that you're normal when you look in the mirror?"

(B) **Harry**: "Let's test it out. Ralph, what do you see when you look in the mirror in the morning?"

(B) **Ralph**: "I see a Black owner of a small marginal business. I know that there are some people out there who have less trust in me because I'm Black. My business with them is going to be done differently just because of the hue of my skin. It impacts me when I go to get a small business loan or try to negotiate a purchase with a wholesaler. Without even intending to, all their images of shifty Negroes, drug dealers, con artists, and perhaps some other prejudices from childhood enter into their interaction with me."

(W) **Jerry**: "I can't believe that. Most people don't think that way, do they? Do the rest of you feel that way?"

(B) **Harry**: "I'm a journalist, Jerry. When that Black New York Times reporter was discovered to be a fraud, I knew that it would affect how other reporters looked at me from that day on. Why do you think it's so important to me to always have my facts right?"

(B) **Felicia**: "Most of us have those fears, Jerry, but it's even worse when you have children."

(W) **Shirley**: "How is that?"

(B) **Felicia**: "Any parent worries about their children getting into trouble, especially when they become teenagers."

(W) **Al**: "Boy, that's the truth. My son just got his driver's license, and I am not sure I have gotten a good night's sleep since then."

(B) **Felicia**: "I understand, Al. But the truth is that my children have a far greater chance than yours do of being stopped as a robbery suspect, and, just because they act like normal, smart-mouthed teenagers, they could be beat up or even killed by well-meaning but scared officers."

(B) **Harry**: "She's right, Al. We have to live with that fear and a sense of powerlessness to protect our children against it everyday."

(W) **Jerry**: "But that's not us. I don't have the power to either do that or not do that."

(B) **Reverend Evan White:** "Of course not, Jerry, but you benefit just because you are white. You don't have to be mean-spirited to benefit from the power of the system."[iii]

UNCONSCIOUS PRIVILEGE

Like most White individuals, White congregations do not normally think of themselves as white. Unless the subject is brought up, they generally think of themselves as *normal congregations*. Most of the racism that affects such congregations remains under the surface and is unconscious. Many such congregations would even rejoice if some people of another ethnic background chose to become members. They might even congratulate themselves on how open and accepting they were.

In recent years a great deal of attention has been given to strategies by which congregations might attract new members to their congregation. Picture the normal response of your congregation if the congregation developed an approach that resulted in a twenty percent growth within two years. Now picture your congregation's response if everything else was the same except that that twenty percent growth was almost totally African Americans.

It is not because White congregations are composed of mean-spirited, prejudiced people. In a similar manner to the personal privileges I described above due to my maleness and height, Caucasians simply live in a society that structures the advantages in their favor. Without even being aware of it, they benefit from the privilege of their "whiteness."

When they turn to a curriculum supply house for educational material, for example, it is rare that the question even arises as to the effect on their children of having most of the people pictured in the curriculum be of a different skin tone from the majority of their members. If they need to acquire a loan for a building program, there may be many problems to resolve, but it is unlikely that they will have to factor in the impact that their race has on those with whom they are negotiating. If they need to settle a zoning issue with respect to their church program, it is more likely that a White congregation will have members who have connections within the larger community to facilitate the resolution of problems that might occur. Their pastors, when they studied in seminary, studied a core theology based on theologians trained in the Western culture. If they did have a class on faith from an African-American or other ethnic background, it was considered an addition to the normal core of faith.

When such pastors accept a call to a congregation, they are not called on to translate such ideas of faith across cultures. Many such issues may seem minor, but cumulatively for African Americans they create an atmosphere of being an outsider always looking in. All ethnic groups face such issues when living in a society dominated by another group, but African Americans carry the additional burden of their ancestors having been slaves and legally considered by the Constitution as less than fully human.

I was in a denominational meeting where a group of clergy and laity were discussing a petition advocating that the church protest the resegregation of the schools that they saw taking place within our communities. There were few in our meeting, Black or White, who would disagree with the concern that was being brought before them. None would have defended returning to segregated schools. However, several of the White people did think that the wording of the petition was too volatile and suggested that it be toned down.

What became apparent was that the White members, without even being conscious of it, were exercising the privilege of their whiteness. If the Black members wanted their protest heard, they would cooperate with the Whites that wanted the language toned down. For the Whites, if the petition was not heard, not a great deal was lost. There is privilege in being able to do nothing and still benefit from it.

THE PRICE OF PRIVILEGE

If Christians who are Caucasian desire to move beyond the plague of racism that has so infected our experience of Christianity in this culture, we need to understand that the redemptive work of God can offer them a sense of hope and a direction in which to move. Many books have been written attempting to analyze the problem of racism in our culture. There also have been a variety of educational and training events designed to help people develop a strategy for dismantling the structures that help perpetuate racism within our society. What we need is a theological framework by which churches can open themselves to the saving work of God with respect to racism.

"My Grace is sufficient for you for
my power is made perfect
in weakness"
2 Corinthians 12: 9

GOD'S VISION FOR GOD'S WORLD

What if God knew the nature of humanity and planned for it in God's redemptive design from the beginning. Assume evil, including the evil of racism, was not a surprise to God or a reality that dictated a series of emergency rescue strategies up to and including the life, death, and resurrection of Christ. If that is accurate, then the coming of Christ was not a radical departure but rather a culminating act by which God seeks to redeem the world. Evils such as racism are clearly actions and conditions that are in rebellion against God and God's intentions for creation, but they are not outside of the redeeming power of God.

In order to explicate this idea, it is necessary to recall the narrative history contained in the Hebrew Scriptures. As the Gospels make clear, what took place in Christ is entirely consistent with what God had already revealed through the Scriptures as to the nature of God's saving work. "Then, beginning with Moses and all the prophets, (Jesus) interpreted to them the things about himself in all the scriptures."[vi]

After they sinned, God clothed Adam and Eve as he sent them from the Garden,[vii] and God would not make an end to the human project in the flood.[viii] God refused to be defeated by evil in the creation. In Genesis 12, the story moves from a story of all of humanity to a more specific story of God with a particular people. However, it is always made clear that the ultimate purpose of God is for the sake of all humanity.[ix]

It is made clear from the beginning that the fulfillment of the promise in the covenant rests on the faithfulness of God and not on the faithfulness or wisdom of humanity.[x] Yet even the Israelites were haunted with the question of whether they might someday cross some invisible line, and God would give up on them. The rather humorous dialogue between God and Moses following the golden calf incident illustrates this fear. God was pictured as so incensed with this act of idolatry that he began to refer to the people not as God's people but as Moses' people. He declared that he was going to wipe them off the face of the earth. It was only Moses' intervention that prevented this judgment from taking place.[xi] Another version of this same question was illustrated in God's rejection of Saul as the chosen one to lead Israel.[xii] God's promise to establish an everlasting covenant with David was an attempt to settle the question of God's faithfulness despite the sinfulness of humanity, but the question still persisted.

While God is a God of justice, as the prophet Hosea described, God's justice is an agonizing struggle with the compassion of God's own heart. "How can I give you up, Ephraim? How can I hand you over, O Israel? How can I make you like Ad'mah? How can I treat you like Zeboi'im? My heart recoils within me; my compassion grows warm and tender. I will not execute my fierce anger; I will not again destroy Ephraim; for I am God and no mortal, the Holy One in your midst, and I will not come in wrath."[xiii]

This compassionate side of God was particularly evident in the life of Israel's greatest hero, David. Among many examples, perhaps the clearest was in the events surrounding his adulterous affair with Bathsheba: murder, adultery, coveting, false witness, stealing. David broke most of the commandments and clearly dishonored God in whose name he had been anointed.

How patient can God be with a person or a people who continue to dishonor him and refuse to recognize their grateful dependence on God? Yet God had made a promise to David, "Your house and your kingdom shall be made sure forever before me; your throne shall be established forever."[xiv] Would God give up on David as God had done with Saul? Will God give up on humanity? If not, how will God's promises be fulfilled in the face of the persistence of human sin?

REDEMPTIVE THEOLOGY

To understand *Redemptive Theology*, we begin with the cross. As Paul said, "For I decided to know nothing among you except Jesus Christ and him crucified."[xv] It is with the cross that the question was answered decisively. The cross revealed the total depravity of humanity while at the same time revealing God's saving response to evil. Recall the story of the incarnation in its most basic narrative form. In the birth of Christ, we experienced Emmanuel or God with us. This was God's son who was sent into the world because God loved the world that God had created and called it good. The cross and the events that led to it were the response of the world to the goodness of God. The cross was a Roman form of execution in order to deter people from disobeying Roman law. It demonstrated Rome's absolute control politically. It also was a cruel, slow, humiliating form of death that was intended to make people fearful of breaking the law. In the story, we see displayed before us the worst insult that humanity could hurl at God.

What would be God's response to the total rejection of God's goodness by humanity? Imagine this story from the purely human perspective. You are a powerful ruler and see some people whose lives are mired in destructive activity. Out of compassion, you send your own child to bring your power to bear on healing their wounds. Instead of being grateful, they kill your son. They even choose to kill him in a painful and insulting manner. This is the basic drama of Scripture. This is the ultimate test of the steadfast love of God.[xvi]

GOD IS NOT DEFEATED BY RACISM

What we discover with the cross is that God is not defeated by evil but is able to work through even the worst displays of human sinfulness to provide a redemptive possibility. The cross, which would have appeared to be the worst sin that humans could commit against the love of God, has become, instead, the very instrument of our redemption. This is the core truth of Redemptive Theology. As God made clear to Paul, "My grace is sufficient for you, for (my) power is made perfect in weakness."

WHAT DID
GOD
KNOW?

RACISM DID NOT SURPRISE GOD

In applying the truth of redemptive theology to the issue of white racism, there are several aspects that need to be noted. **First**, *Redemptive Theology* assumes that God is omniscient and therefore knew from the beginning the nature of humanity and the effect of sin on God's creative purpose. God knows the nature of the church, and the sin of racism. God calls the church into reality within this culture. God knows from the beginning that racism is a part of the American culture and therefore a critical aspect of the community of faith within which God is working God's saving work.

GOD IS NOT DEFEATED BY A SINFUL CHURCH

Second, Redemptive Theology also assumes that God is omnipotent and is not defeated by sin but intentionally incorporates the reality of sin into God's plan of salvation. For example, when David was confronted with his sin by God's prophet, Nathan, David did not live in denial but confessed his sin before God. For narrative purposes, the canon saw Psalm 51 as an expression of David's confession before God. Humanity suffers for their sins and the sins of others, as seen in the death of Bathsheba's child and would later be seen in the disintegration of David's family, but God can transform even sin into a redeeming possibility. David and Bathsheba have another son, Solomon. This son will provide the family line from which Christ will be born. Matthew emphasized this aspect of God's redeeming work in the genealogy with which he began his gospel. In contrast to most genealogies, Matthew not only includes women but makes a point of including women such as Bathsheba who had questionable qualities in their lives. God can use even the sin of adultery for a greater purpose.

DON'T DENY REALITY

With respect to racism, God's saving work within the church is not experienced by denying the reality of racism. With the cross as our template, we seek to understand how God can transform racism into God's saving work. There is hope not because racism is insignificant but because God is not defeated by it. If God can use our response to racism for healing, there is hope for a fractured world.

DON'T BE PARALYZED BY GUILT

Third, Redemptive Theology also assumes the holiness of God. God is a God of justice who cannot simply overlook the sins of humanity as if they were unimportant in God's larger plan. God has created a moral universe in which humanity must be held accountable for its behavior. However, God is also responsible for the creatures that God has created and cannot allow them to be destroyed by the sinful possibilities of their nature. Therefore, racism within God's church cannot be ignored, but needs to be confessed. In most White congregations, racism is a reality that is not talked about or even acknowledged. In churches that do take it seriously, there is often a tendency to become paralyzed with an overwhelming sense of guilt that results in what is often referred to as "white bashing." Neither response is especially helpful in moving towards a healthier future.

WE DON'T EDUCATE OURSELVES TO SALVATION

Fourth, Redemptive Theology acknowledges the inability of humanity to save itself. While we may educate ourselves to the dimensions of sin, such as racism, and may draw upon the techniques of behavioral psychology to alter behavior and attitudes, Christian hope does not depend upon human progress for salvation with respect to this or any sin.

One does not have to read much about the history of racism within our society to recognize the insidious ability that racism has to infuse every aspect of our personal and corporate lives. It repeatedly morphs into new forms in defiance of our attempts to eradicate it. One of those forms is the continual effort of the dominant culture to assert that we are progressively triumphing over the effects of racism. No significant sacrifices in our lives are necessary to achieve a society free of racism.

TRUST THAT GOD TRANSFORMS

Fifth, Redemptive Theology places its trust in the creative power of God who not only is not defeated by evil but also is able to take even the worst of evils and transform it into a redemptive possibility. With respect to racism, this means that while it is an evil scourge on our churches, in the hands of God it can be transformed into a redemptive possibility.

RECONCILIATION CELEBRATES GOD'S LOVE OF DIVERSITY

Redemptive Theology is rooted in an affirmation of God's intention for creation. Whether it be in creation itself or in the separation of the androgynous creature into sexually specific male and female, life is the result of division that leaves a yearning for reconciliation. God also yearns for that reconciliation. "God was in Christ reconciling the world to Godself…" Such reconciliation is not the homogenization of our differences but a celebration of the richness of our differences that enrich the whole.

> "To each is given
> the manifestation of the Spirit
> for the common good."
> 1 Corinthians 12:7

Sixth

For Christians, this is most clearly depicted in the economy of the Trinity. God, Christ, and the Spirit live in relationship to each other in perfect harmony and yet with appreciation of the distinctiveness of each. The variety within our creation, including races, was part of God's intention in preparation for the full reconciliation with the divine. Our inability to relate to each other with appreciation and respect for our differences demonstrates our distance from God who is utterly different from any of us. It is only as we learn to live in the midst of the diversity of creation with rejoicing in the otherness of those who are different from us that we can grow closer to God. Full reconciliation in a world that can celebrate the beauty of our diversity prepares us to gaze upon the beauty of God.

RECOGNIZE THE CHURCH'S SCANDAL

For Christians to respond to the reality of racism in our lives and in our congregations, we must first move beyond denial. In classic Christian terminology, "If we say that we have no sin, we deceive ourselves, and the truth is not in us." But such confession is done in hope. "If we confess our sins, he who is faithful and just will forgive us our sins and cleanse us from all unrighteousness." A congregation that desires to overcome the sin of racism that bogs down and distorts their experience of the faith must begin with confession. Such a confession can be seen as a positive step. It is a significant step towards the healing of a major division among humanity.

GET OUT OF PRISON

Of course, just because you confess, forgiveness by the victimized humans is not inevitable. Desmond Tutu relates a story of the cost to the victim that will not forgive. "A recent issue of the journal Spirituality and Health had on its front cover a picture of three U.S. ex-servicemen standing in front of the Vietnam memorial in Washington, D.C. One asks, 'Have you forgiven those who held you prisoner of war?' 'I will never forgive them,' replies the other. His mate says: 'Then it seems they still have you in prison, don't they?'"

LISTENING TO THE STORY

Tutu continues, "In forgiving, people are not being asked to forget. On the contrary, it is important to remember, so that we should not let such atrocities happen again. Forgiveness does not mean condoning what has been done. It means taking what happened seriously and not minimizing it." Forgiveness draws out the sting in the memory that threatens to poison our entire existence."

One of the powerful discoveries in the *Truth and Reconciliation Commission* in South Africa was the power of truth-telling. There was healing in the victims finally having someone listen to their story of suffering and honoring their pain. Desmond Tutu notes, "It may be, for instance, that race relations in the United States will not improve significantly until Native Americans and African Americans get the opportunity to tell their stories and reveal the pain that sits in the pit of their stomachs as a baneful legacy of dispossession and slavery."

RECOVERING RACISTS

For a White congregation to move to the step of confessing that they are racist is neither an easy step nor does it, in itself, solve the problem of racism. To draw upon the truth discovered in Alcoholics Anonymous, White people and White congregations are always "recovering racists." That is as much a given of our context as being an alcoholic is a given of their reality. We did not create the history that shaped us, but we cannot escape it either. A critical step in our healing, however, is acknowledgment of the problem.

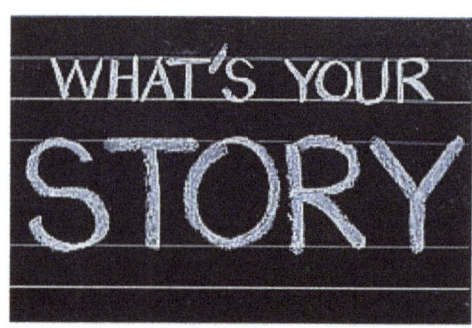

SAVED TO COMMUNITY

In God's economy, we are saved to community. We not only need to confess, but we need someone to listen to our confession. Picture the power of members of a White congregation taking the sin of racism so seriously that they are willing to sit before a Black congregation and listen intensely to the pain that their African-American neighbors experience in their lives. Consider the healing of Black members hearing White Christians confess to complicity in the sin of racism. "True forgiveness deals with the past, all of the past, to make the future possible."

Such confession is not a single act but a process. We continue to need the dialogue made available through community. While individual congregations may be of predominantly one race, the Body of Christ is diverse. Thus, God's gift of the church to humanity is to provide humanity with that community of faith that transcends human divisions and provides it a context for such a dialogue.

OWN OUR HELPLESSNESS

Continuing with the model provided for us by Alcoholics Anonymous, the second step of the process is to admit our helplessness to control this disease and our dependence on a higher power. While education is important, we cannot educate ourselves out of racism. While laws to protect the community are important, we cannot legislate the end of racism. The history of racism makes it clear that racism will not be defeated by human agency alone.

Our hope lies in the redemptive power of God that has been revealed in the cross. The cross revealed that God is not defeated by evil and can use the experience of evil redemptively. Not even racism can defeat God's reconciling purpose for humanity. If racism is our cross, the rebellious act by which we defy the intention of God, our hope is that God can use this cross as part of God's redemptive purpose.

It is important to emphasize that this is not an attempt to justify the evil of racism or to suggest that it is good in disguise. Evil is evil, but God is neither restrained nor defeated by it. As Christians have learned through the ages, however, we must turn and face the cross if we are to experience its redemptive power. "Who was the guilty? Who brought this upon you? It is my treason, Lord that has undone you. 'Twas I, Lord Jesus, I it was denied you; I crucified you." ("Ah, Holy Jesus) We not only do not need to deny the corporate history of racism in our nation and in our church and the ways that we have benefited from it, but it is important that we turn and acknowledge it for our own salvation.

RECOGNIZING WHITE PRIVILEGE

By identifying the types of privileges that have come to us by virtue of our being white, we can share in the search for the signs of God working redemptively in those very areas. God's frequent pattern in Scripture is to work through less than pure people.

Jesus followers held clear prejudices. "The disciples rebuked those who brought the children for Jesus' blessing (Matt.19:13). They were surprised to see Jesus speaking to a Samaritan woman (John 4:27). These same twelve beseeched Jesus to send the woman of Canaan away when she sought healing (Matt. 15:23). Prejudice toward children, Samaritans, and Canaanites influenced the disciples' response in each instance. Yet Jesus worked through them to heal the oppression of prejudice. It is easy to demonstrate, through the history of the church, that we continue to be filled with prejudice. When Jesus is quoted in Luke 19:10 as saying, "For the Son of Man came to seek out and to save the lost," it is important for the church not to shy away from the truth that Jesus is referring to us.

If the process of confession and forgiveness between Black and White congregations takes place, God can then liberate them to seek signs of God's redemptive power at work in the whole Body of Christ. Economic benefits and societal acceptance, for example, are strengths that can be utilized for the good of the whole. Could not such economic privileges, political power, managerial abilities, and shared theological truths contribute to a strategy by which the structures of racism in the larger society might be confronted?

THE SUFFERING SERVANT MODEL

Of course, trying to address the demonic power of racism in the society is not an easy task. This is where it is important that the believers be joined together in community and be well-grounded in the faith. God's story, as revealed in the cross, is an invitation to the privilege of sacrifice and will likely include both great effort and not a little measure of suffering. It was not pleasant for Jesus to go to the cross. His invitation to his followers to take up the cross and follow him was not meant to be an invitation to luxurious comfort. Jesus deliberately chose the path of the suffering servant and invites us to participate in this path by which God is glorified.

However, it was not an invitation to suffering for suffering's sake. What lifts this type of suffering beyond mere pain is that it is a suffering for a greater purpose. Many people in the course of their lives have experienced the nobility of suffering for a greater purpose. Athletes strain their body in order to achieve a team victory. Soldiers sacrifice their lives for their country. Scientists spend long hours seeking to make a discovery that will benefit others. Jesus offers us the opportunity to devote ourselves to the greatest purpose of all. We are invited to participate in the life of the suffering servant and share in the reconciliation of the world.

AN INVITATION TO TRUST A REDEMPTIVE GOD

Using the cross and the resurrection as our template for how God works in our world, congregations are invited to face the evil of the cross of racism, trusting that God is not defeated by such evil, and to search for ways that God can use even the reality of racism redemptively.

It is important to approach this search for the redemptive power of God with a combination of faith and humility. The Gospels recount that Jesus told his disciples three times that he would be crucified and would be raised from the dead. Despite Jesus having said this, it is clear that the disciples did not understand what this meant. They had to live the truth of the resurrection before they could understand it. We can believe that racism will be used redemptively, but we must live the truth of God's redemptive power to discover its full meaning.

REPARATIONS

One aspect of God's reconciling work may involve the issue of reparation. Desmond Tutu, in speaking about the struggle to overcome racism in South Africa, speaks of the challenge of reparations. To "put the past behind us" and act as if an act of confession clears the tables of justice and allows us to "get on with life" is to trivialize the pain of the past. Part of our painful past is the fact that our constitution clearly states that our ancestors were fully aware of the economic value of slave labor in building a prosperous country. Historically, both Native Americans and African Americans paid a heavy price for the economic prosperity of this country. There is no way that one could calculate the value to African Americans in lives and wealth that racism has cost their ancestors. While there may be efforts to make symbolic economic reparation, as we have done with respect to Native Americans and to the Japanese Americans that we imprisoned during World War II, it would not be feasible to actually restore to a current generation that which has been taken from their ancestors. However, if we fully explore the various dimensions of that cost together, can God use our confession of sins redemptively? For example, can God raise our awareness to respond to the challenge posed by the new wave of immigration in our country?

PSYCHIC COST OF SLAVERY

There is also no clear way to calculate the psychic cost passed down through generations of African Americans with respect to the heritage of slavery that was imposed on them. The issue of the disproportionate incarceration of African-American males in our society might well be the result of a combination of the current prejudice of courts, police, but, also, the historic psychic cost in which victims begin to accept the judgment of the dominant society. If Black and White congregations were willing to explore that reality together, perhaps another form of reparation might be the focus of energy on the redemption of those who are in prison in our society. It would be a way that the Body of Christ could embody Jesus' statement about his own ministry, "He has sent me to proclaim release to the captives and recovery of sight to the blind, to let the oppressed go free, to proclaim the year of the Lord's favor."

Caucasian people rarely think of themselves as belonging to a race, but Black people are rarely allowed to forget they are distinct. Consider the following questions from the perspective of your racial identity. Think of your family experience and mark each question with F for frequently, O for occasionally, R for rarely or never. As you mark your chart, note the feelings that such answers generate in you and the feelings that your overall score generates in you.

Fill out the questions as individuals and then begin to record the cumulative scores of the Caucasian participants and of the Black participants.

1. Were my parents or other family members treated unfairly or badly because of the color of their skin?

2. Have I noticed someone lock the doors of their car, because they saw me near by?

3. Have I been stopped by police because I was driving in a neighborhood different from mine?

4. Have the police accused me or family members of having or selling drugs?

5. Has someone misunderstood my intentions and motives, because of my race?

6. Have I seen someone cross the street because of my race?

7. Have people looked at me with suspicion, because of my race?

8. Have I or family members been watched closely or followed around by security guards or store clerks at a store or mall?

9. Have I or family members been talked down to because of race?

10. How many times have I or family members been asked to speak for my race?

11. Has someone assumed I fit a stereotype of my race? (have rhythm, play sports, have loose morals, etc.)

12. Have I been mistaken for someone else because of my race?

13. Have I heard someone refer to people of 'your culture' or 'background' in a negative way?

14. Have I or a family member been treated unfairly by people in service jobs (store clerks, waiters, bartenders, bank tellers and others)?

15. Have I or family members received poor service at a restaurant, because of our race?

16. How many times did someone discourage us from trying to achieve an important goal, because of our race?

17. Has anyone acted as if I was dishonest, because of my race?

18. How many times have family members encountered people who were surprised that, given our race or ethnic background, we did something really well?

19. How many times did someone ignore you or exclude one of us from activities, because of our race?

20. How many times have I or family members been called bad names, because of our race?

21. How many times have we felt out of place in a social situation because of our race?

Individuals can take the test for their own awareness, but it will be more effective if it is taken in a group. Have each member calculate the total score for how many items were marked with an F, O, or R. Then have people share their scores and how it impacts how they feel.

Avoid the temptation of individuals wanting to explain or comment on the individual questions. While individual questions might be interpreted differently, the purpose is to raise an awareness of the cumulative impact of race in our society.

These questions can make any of us feel uncomfortable. The intention is not to raise the level of guilt or embarrassment, but to raise our consciousness of how even small events can be impacted sometimes by overt and sometimes by subtle reminders of the place of race in our society.

You might ask people to comment on how it makes them feel to hear the scores of the other group? And how it makes them feel to have this experience in a mixed group?

GOD'S HISTORY OF SURPRISES

To approach the problem of racism from the perspective of a redemptive God is to both acknowledge our sins and be open to God's saving activity. The Scriptures continually report that God is full of surprises from a human perspective. Redemptive Theology anticipates the exciting possibility that God might use the very troubling experiences we have had with racism as an opportunity to advance the reconciling possibilities in our world. In taking this path, we are learning to live with the diversity of God's creation in a way that enhances all of its parts. Our model is the Trinity. Each part is distinctive, all are equal, and each contributes to the good of the whole. As we evolve in our capacity to live in the rich diversity of the world, we prepare ourselves to experience communion with the God who created all of us and calls us home.

Desmond Tutu speaks of the cost to the privileged in South Africa. "All South Africans were less whole than we would have been without apartheid. Those who were privileged lost out as they became more uncaring, less compassionate, less humane, and therefore less human; . . ." *No Future without Forgiveness; Desmond Tutu; Doubleday; 1999; page 196*

SEEING AND TRUSTING IN GOD'S CONSUMATING WILL

The Consummating Will of God refers to the intention that God has had from the beginning of creation and will accomplish by the end of time. This intention is in contrast to the Gnostic assumption that creation is basically evil and that God's saving work is to enable the faithful to be "raptured" out of this evil world. It also stands as a challenge to a belief that while God created the world as "good," it has become so hopelessly defiant of God's goodness that in desperation God sent Christ to redeem the world. The Consummating Will of God sees the act of Christ's coming, death, and resurrection as part of a plan of salvation that God intended from the beginning and will bring to fulfillment in the end.

FOOT NOTES

[i] It has become common to refer to such congregations as "predominantly white" to acknowledge that many such congregations will have some members from other ethnic backgrounds. I will refer to such congregations as "white" because this is the dominant culture in which they operate even though I recognize that there might be some representation of other ethnic backgrounds in their membership. I will be speaking as a white clergyperson about White congregations.

[ii] I will capitalize "White" and "Black" when they refer to people who are Caucasian or Negro. I realize that race is more an accepted designation than a scientific reality. However, in our society, they have become powerful designations often with tragic consequences.

[iii] Excerpted from *The Color of Bread*, written by Dr. Samuel Stevenson and Stephen P. McCutchan

[iv] Desmond Tutu speaks of the cost to the privileged in South Africa. "All South Africans were less whole than we would have been without apartheid. Those who were privileged lost out as they became more uncaring, less compassionate, less humane, and therefore less human; . . ." *No Future without Forgiveness;* Desmond Tutu; Doubleday; 1999; page 196

[v] The Consummating Will of God refers to the intention that God has had from the beginning of creation and will accomplish by the end of time. This intention is in contrast to the Gnostic assumption that creation is basically evil and that God's saving work is to enable the faithful to be "raptured" out of this evil world. It also stands as a challenge to a belief that while God created the world as "good," it has become so hopelessly defiant of God's goodness that in desperation God sent Christ to redeem the world.

[vi] Luke 24:27. All four gospels insist on making the point that what happened to Jesus was consistent with the nature of God that had been previously revealed in the Hebrew Scriptures.

[vii] Genesis 3:21.

[viii] Genesis 6:1-9:17

[ix] Genesis 12:3b

[x] Genesis 15:1-21. In this earliest narrative of the covenant between God and Abram, it was the smoking fire pot, a symbol for God, and not Abram who passed through the cut-up pieces of the animals. Normally in such covenant making ceremonies, both parties would pass through the split animals.

[xi] Genesis 32:7-14

[xii] 1 Samuel 13:5-14

[xiii] Hosea 11:8-9

[xiv] 2 Samuel 7:16.

[xv] 1 Corinthians 2:2

[xvi] Matthew 21:33-42. Note that in this story it is the common assumption of the listeners that the owner will respond with violence to the people's insult because that is the way the world thinks. Jesus, however, challenges their response with, "Have you never read in the scriptures: 'The very stone which the builders rejected has become the head of the corner; this was the Lord's doing, and it is marvelous in our eyes.'"

HOW DO YOU DISCUSS RACE IN MIXED COMPANY

Ok, so you've taken a significant step in establishing a connection with another community that is of a predominantly different racial background than your community. Perhaps you've had a couple of joint congregational suppers, some choir and pulpit exchanges, but how do you add more depth to your relationship. You want to get beyond being polite to each other and have a deeper conversation, but how?

I want to call your attention to how Jesus used parables. If you want examples of artful flash fiction, review some of Jesus' parables. Jesus' parables were short fictional stories that built on familiar settings but often had some unique twists that caused people to stop and think about fresh perspectives. In less than 320 words (an English version), Jesus engaged his listeners in probing our response to violence, bigotry, and hypocrisy in the parable of the Good Samaritan. In approximately 200 words, Jesus probed the destructive impact of materialism in the parable of the Rich Fool. In just a little over 100 words, Jesus paints a picture of the effort God will go to in recovering those who have lost their way in this world. (Luke 12:3-7.) While we may not be as good a storyteller as Jesus, I want to propose that we follow the same practice.

People are nervous when they talk about race, particularly in mixed company (double entendre intended.) By writing fiction, particularly under the duress of time pressures, we can safely explore subjects in fresh ways.

The process is that you will provide participants with several scenarios which involve racial challenges. You will also provide brief sketches of two characters who will engage in conversation within the context of the scene provided, with particular emphasis on the ways that racial understandings infuse the conversation. Emphasize that the characters have both positive and negative attitudes in their conversation.

Once the scenarios are distributed, people are to begin with the sentence provided and create a dialogue that might take place between the characters. In some cases, they may express tension of interpersonal understanding, but in other cases, they may be allying against some societal situation. They will have only thirty minutes to write and will not be able to complete their parable.

At the end of the writing period, people will gather in small interracial groups and share and discuss their stories. The discomfort of speaking about race may well be eased by the shared discomfort of being pushed to write so quickly. The pressure to write without stopping to think can result in some new ideas surfacing. The responsibility for those thoughts belong to the characters and not the author.

The church is filled with diversity. Wouldn't it be wonderful if the larger society looked at what we do and responded, "See how they love each other."

This booklet offers one sample scenario that can be used, but you are encouraged to choose your own theme, name and describe two or three characters, and a scene in which the action begins. Then release your imagination and that of other participants and make the stories the basis for deeper conversation.

GAINING NEW MEMBERS

Setting: A modest size church (either predominantly Caucasian or African American —the opposite of the writer). The church has experienced a slight decline in membership the past few years.

Precipitating event: Because of a new housing development, many new residents have moved into the community. The church has had a reputation for being dynamic, and many of the new residents are attracted to the services.
It becomes evident that fifty or more families from a contrasting ethnic identity of the dominant population of the church are interested in joining.

Dialogue characters: *Ralph Johnson:*

Major figure in the church. Sixty years of age, married to Ethel, who is also active in the church. Both have been members for thirty years and very influential in church decision making. He is a modest businessman in his community and tends to prefer calm and steady approaches to life.

Scott Berkshire:

He has been pastor of the church for the past five years. He is mildly liberal but always concerned about pleasing all members and avoiding conflict. He is married and has two children in elementary school. He is a good preacher and extrovertish personality. He takes his faith quite seriously and values his integrity.

YOUR TASK:The subject is race, prejudice, and racism. Read your scenario, add one or two characteristics to each dialogue character—physical, emotional, social, past history, etc.

Begin to write the dialogue among the characters listed. Avoid stereotypes. Allow each of your characters to display positive and negative qualities and to show both understanding and prejudice in their conversation.

Ralph: "Pastor, I'm not prejudice, but don't you think that fifty new families who are different from most of our congregation is going to cause a major upset?"

Agree upon a time framework within which all participants will write their scene. The value of a time pressure, say less than one half-hour, is that everyone recognizes that grammar, style, and elaborate descriptions are not relevant to the task. This liberates people to just allow their imagination to guide them.

Give yourselves permission to have fun
even as you are confronting
a complex and difficult issue.

TRUTH AND RECONCILIATION

What if we restructured the "Truth and Reconciliation" process and applied it to how we move beyond racism in our society? Since it came out of a violent moment in South African history, a reframed experience could identify the truth of the violence in this society and move beyond abstraction to deal with the violence and bigotry.

We acknowledge the shame of our country's history which includes all non-Caucasians but we begin with a focus on Black people. We challenge Caucasians to come, as they did in South Africa, and confess their participation in a culture of privilege. They may confess to particular actions (or non-actions) on their part but include their feelings of shame about their *race* having benefited from the world as it was structured.

They make that confession in the company of Blacks who have gathered. When it is their turn, Black participants are offered the opportunity to confess why it is difficult to offer forgiveness but also any hopes they see contained in the power they now have in offering such forgiveness.

THE CHURCH'S TRUTH AND RECONCILIATION COMMISSION

WHY WOULD PEOPLE WANT TO RISK BEING PARTICIPANTS OF THE TRC FOR CHURCHES?

First, faithful to our commission to be ambassadors of reconciliation, the church is inviting those who have suffered the price of systemic racism to join the church in seeking God's healing. (2 COR 5:20)

Second, the whole church has suffered from the sin of racism and needs healing.

Third, our society has been infected by racism and needs to discover a path to hope and healing.

Fourth, God is praised when people permit themselves to be faithful on behalf of God's beloved world.

LEVELS OF PARTICIPATION

If a church is integrated, they may want to begin with the members of the one church and then seek to share their experience with both other churches and the world. If a church's membership is predominantly of one race, they can seek the participation of another church whose membership is of another race. In this example, we are addressing race relationships between Black and White membership.

While non-Christians are invited to participate, the exercise acts from an overt Christian perspective. However, it needs to be recognized that there are diverse definitions of that perspective.

There are four ways that people can participate.

1. There needs to be a leadership body representing both churches.
2. Ideally people who address the TRC will do it personally at a public meeting.
3. If someone wants to share their story but is reluctant to appear publicly, they can write their story and submit it to the leadership.
4. An audience of non-participants can attend the public meeting.

The key factor is learning how to listen with both heart and mind.

THE FRAMEWORK FOR THE MEETINGS

Members of the leadership will provide a comfortable and safe setting at which they will interview and listen to those who wish to tell their story.

Where appropriate, they will provide a person from the team to accompany the speaker and offer support.

An individual who wishes to speak will be placed on a schedule and permitted to speak without interruption for an agreed upon period of time. While the leadership may pose questions for clarification, no challenges or judgments are acceptable.

There is a two-fold perspective for the conversations and an umbrella purpose.

1. Black participants are asked to share the story of their experience with racism in their life that includes both what it was like growing up in our society and any specific incidents that they desire to describe. Included in their story should both be the factual description and the emotional impact on their development.
2. White participants speak on a more confessional level. They are asked to both describe their level of awareness of White privilege and the impact it has had on them as they increasingly recognize how it impacts their Black neighbors.

The umbrella purpose is to submit to the hope that with confession and forgiveness, there is a God given potential to advance the reconciliation and enrichment of humanity.

The TRC for churches follows a four-fold framework.

1. People who have been hurt in human interaction can move from victimhood to healed purpose and meaning in life through being able to tell their story.
2. That process permits them to name the hurts they have experienced. Having given voice to their hurts and knowing it has been heard opens them to the possibility of being liberated to discover their *true self* as God would intend.
3. This offers the opportunity for the offending population to seek forgiveness for the wounding context of which they have been a part.
4. If such confession is both voiced and forgiveness given, then there is the possibility of renewed connection where there had been division. A witness to a richer world that draws upon all the gifts God has offered is advanced.

While the pain of injustice is real, the church's faith invites us to move from getting revenge for our hurt to being open to a restoration of a relationship that could have been. We move from retributive justice (making them pay) to restorative justice (healing the brokenness of community).

We also move from denial to acceptance of our part in the imbalance of community. While I didn't own any slaves, nor do I deliberately conspire to discriminate or treat unjustly people who are different from me, I do benefit from a variety of conditions in both my history and my present context. A major factor in this imbalance is the distribution of power within the community.

THE STRUCTURE OF THE MEETING

The leadership convenes the meeting with a prayer to God to both hear our pain and our stories and to bless us with restorative options.

Next, four or five Blacks share their stories, including both facts and emotions, as to their life's experience. The stories are received without judgement or question except for clarification.

Then, two or three Whites, not directly addressing the previous stories, confess to their awareness of the benefits they have experience in life and any sense of responsibility they recognize for not challenging racists conditions or advocating for greater healing in their immediate lives or their larger community.

This rotation of speakers continues within the time framework established. Other written stories are also distributed.

Phase 1 is concluded with prayer for forgiveness and healing.

Phase 2 begins with prayer.

People who desire are permitted an opportunity to voice confession and or forgiveness.

Next, the group begins to explore tentative ideas of how they might write a new corporate story for the Christian community. Any participants who desire may write a paragraph painting a vision of what the Christian community might look like beyond the division of racism.

AND I WILL SHOW YOU
A MORE EXCELLENT WAY